Energy Vampires:

Managing stress & Negative thoughts In your Personal & Professional Life.

Dr. Steve Ornelas

Copyright © 2007 by Steve Ornelas

Published and bound in the United States of America. All rights reserved. No part of this book may be reproduced by any photographic, mechanical, or electronic process. Nor in the form of a phonographic recording, stored in a retrieval system, or transmitted. It cannot be copied for public or private use, except for "fair use" or as brief quotations used in articles and reviews without prior written consent of the publisher.

The author of this book and the information provided by GabSum Productions LLC or in their workshops is neither intended nor implied to be a substitute for professional medical advice. You should not use this information or the information from the presenters to diagnose or treat a health problem, emotional, or diseases without consulting with a qualified healthcare provider. Medical information obtained from this book or workshops is not intended as a substitute for professional care. If you have or suspect you have a problem, you should consult a healthcare provider. The intent of the author is only to offer information of a general nature to help you in your quest for emotional and spiritual well-being.

In no event shall GabSum Productions LLC or its presenters be liable for any damage arising, directly or indirectly, from the use of the information contained on this workshop, including damages arising from inaccuracies, omissions, errors or copyright infringement. GabSum Productions LLC and its representatives are not responsible or liable for any advice, course of treatment, diagnosis, or any other information, or service.

For information, contact GabSum Productions LLC, 3016 E. Wildwood Dr., Phoenix, AZ. 85048 or email at sornelasphd@msn.com.

ISBN# 978-0-6151-7435-8

Ornelas, Steve
	Energy Vampires: Managing stress & Negative thoughts in your personal & professional life. By Dr, Steve Ornelas.

Dedication

*This book is dedicated to my mom & dad, Laura & Edward Ornelas.
I thank you both for your unyielding love and support throughout my life!
Through you, I learned the love of life, education, dreams, faith, and Family.
You have always been and always will be my greatest example of the positive energy that comes from unconditional love!
I was blessed to have you both as parents and role models!
THANK YOU!*

Table of Contents

Preface……………………………………..…………………….5
Introduction: Life is a classroom………………....…..……..10

Be Mindful that you are a Student of Life……………….........12
Be Mindful that you are a Teacher of life……………….…..16
Be Mindful that you have "freedom of choice."…………...…..16
Be Mindful of your Energy Investments..……………………..18

Step 1: Become Mindful of your personal boundaries &
        responsibilities………………………….………21
- The Savior Syndrome…………………….…26
- Are you a people pleaser?.......................................27

Step 2: Become Mindful of the "Energy Vampires" in your
        life………………………………………………..30
- What are Energy Vampires & who are yours?.....30
- Who & what is draining you of your energy or
  spirit?..31
- Plan your reactions…………….………….…33
- External energy drains……………………...…34
- Internal energy drains……………...…………35
- Beware of the "Emotional Black Holes"?............37
- What does your personal energy
  universe look like..............................38
- Exercise 1: Your personal energy universe ….....41
- If life were a movie, are you living
  a drama or comedy?........................43
- Exercise 2: Write your own personal movie
  script………..…………………...44

Step 3: Become Mindful of your Islands of Stability………..45
- See the storms in your life as opportunities……..45
- Identify the positive people in your life………..47
- Exercise 3: Identify your islands of stability…….48
- External Islands of stability…………………...48
- Internal Islands of stability……..……………49
- So what to do when confronted by an EV……….50

About the Author……………………………………...…53

Preface

"You are enrolled in a full-time informal school called Life. Each day in this school you will have the opportunity to learn lessons. You may like the lessons or think them irrelevant and stupid."
- Cherie Carter-Scott

So how did I come up with this title and content of this book? Good question. The "Energy Vampire" Book, also known as the first three steps, was written in preparation for a faculty in-service with the main goal of helping participants become more "Mindful" of the connection between their personal/professional life and the energy vampires in each. Energy Vampires are those people, situations, or things in your life that drain you of your energy. It is very important to take time to recognize who and what are the energy vampires in your life, both at home and at work. If you are not aware of them, then they can suck you dry of your vital life force.

The "Energy Vampires" book is the first part of a bigger series called "Life's Little Box of Chocolates; Enjoy the Flavors of Life. I came up with the series with a total of 9 steps as a part of my life coaching practice. I start my new clients/students off by asking them what are their purpose and their philosophy of life. In trying to figure out how to explain what a "philosophy of life" was, I came up with describing a "philosophy of life" as the way you see the world and approach the situations of life. As Forrest Gump's Mama would say..."Life is like a box of chocolates…you never know what you are going to get." I have to agree! You never know what you will get in life and rule #1 is that "Life isn't always fair." The most important thing is how you choose to react to life's situations.

Life's situations are like the chocolate candies in the box of life. They vary within flavor, texture, and experience. The question is "what will you do if you get a piece of chocolate you weren't expecting and didn't like?" Will you toss it out and try for another one? Are you the type of person who picks certain ones because of their shape or color of the chocolate? Do you dive into the box of chocolates with reckless abandon and try the first chocolate you see? Or will you take your time to pick just the right one. How would you approach "Life's Little Box of Chocolates?"

"Life's Little Box of Chocolates" reflects a person's philosophy of life or their approach to Life. Like a box of chocolates, there are so many different types and flavors of candies in one box. Some pieces are milky and smooth while another may be hard and chewy. The first book with the title "Life's Little Box of Chocolates" was a compilation of emails that have come across my computer. I hope that the emails would touch you as well. In a sense, the emails can be considered little tastes of life. So I encourage you to please enjoy and dig into "Life's little box of chocolates and experience the flavors of Life: Email Edition."

The current edition of Life's Little Box of Chocolates; Experiencing the Flavors of Life: "The 9 Steps to Finding Peace and Balance in Your Personal & Professional Life" was written as a way of helping my personal coaching students as well as my college students. I see life as the ultimate classroom. My main goal is to apply my years of teaching and the lessons I've learned from life to help my students learn from their own experiences.

The "Energy Vampires" contains the first 3 steps of this book which have some exercises to help you assess your personal energy universe by identifying the negative and positive people in your life. By finding out and recognizing what or who drains you of your spiritual energy, you become more capable of managing your time and energy to become more productive and find more peace in life.

The second set of 3 steps (steps 4, 5, & 6) focus on being mindful of controlling how you think, feel, and behave. By first recognizing what you are thinking and feeling, you will be better able to understand and control your behavior. The last 3 steps (steps 7, 8, & 9) discuss who you are, how you have been programmed (Life Script) and finally, how to re-write your life script.

By learning from your experiences and reading this book, you begin to really live life on a conscious level instead of living life asleep and reactive. The entire book of the 9 steps is separated into thirds. The first three steps focus on identifying Personal Boundaries, Energy Vampires, Islands of Stability and discussing them as a part of your life. The second set of three steps focuses on being mindful of and controlling how you think, feel, and behave. The last three steps focus on understanding who you are, where your life scripts came from, and how you can begin to re-write your life script for yourself. By following the 9 steps, you will take control of your life by controlling how you think, feel, and behave and making your life what you have always dreamed.

I hope that you will enjoy this first edition of the book and find it helpful. The purpose of my books and workshops is to "Open hearts and minds through quality educational experiences, and more importantly…to Have FUN!"

Introduction

Steps to finding peace & balance in the "classroom" of Life.

"When the student is ready, the lessons appear"
- Gene Oliver (Former American Baseball player b1935)

**Life is a classroom:
There are Lessons to be learned in every situation...
If you are willing to learn!**

"A life spent making mistakes is not only more honorable, but more useful than a life spent doing nothing."
- George Bernard Shaw

One of the first things I share with my students is my philosophy of teaching and of life. "Life" is the ultimate classroom. It gives us many opportunities to learn from our experiences. We are all teachers and students of life. There are lessons all around giving us opportunities to grow and to learn about ourselves. If we only choose to listen and learn, we can be more open to the "teachable moments" in life and benefit from their lessons.

In my psychology classes, I stress that the best learning comes from the personal application of the material covered in class and visa versa. If there is a personal experience or meaning attached, it helps in storing the new information in long term memory. This is why I bring to life the concepts and definitions covered in our readings. If you can attach a meaning to an experience, you will remember it more. This is why even negative experiences are hard to forget. I will discuss later how to deal with these wounds of the spirit caused by negative experiences. The goal in life is to learn the lessons needed to spiritually grow by putting what you have learned into action. Always remember, knowledge for knowledge sake is really worthless until you apply it or it causes some type of change in behavior.

    The idea of "knowledge" as the basic step in the learning theory fits with Benjamin Bloom's (1956) theory classifying levels of intellectual behavior. His theory ranges from a simple recall or recognition of facts (knowledge or rote memory) as the lowest level, through a more increasingly complex and abstract mental levels. The highest order on the Bloom's list is classified as evaluation. During the 1990's, a new group of cognitive psychologists lead by a former student of Bloom's Lorin Anderson (2000), changed the basic level from "knowledge" to "remembering," with understanding, applying, analyzing, evaluating, and creating finishing off the pyramid. (see below)

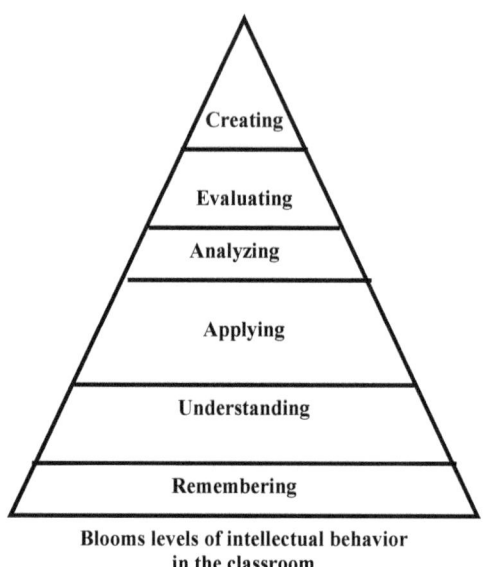

Blooms levels of intellectual behavior in the classroom

<u>*Be Mindful that you are a Student of Life:*</u>

"Who dares to teach must never cease to learn."
- *John Cotton Dana*

You can apply the terms from Bloom's Taxonomy in the formal educational classroom to the lessons we learn from life's situations. One such example, the first level of learning, is "remembering" and in life it can be called "conditioning," "rote memory" or "life script." The five upper levels fit the learning from life's classroom model and are needed in order to live life consciously and become an active learner of life. An active learner is one who is actively engaged and participating in life and not just sitting back and reacting to life's situations. Being a "passive learner" in life means you are generally a receiver of knowledge and rely primarily on conditioning and rote learning. When you are an active learner of life, you will not stay stuck in the lowest level of conditioning or rote memory. (see below) As an active learner of life, you will begin to work your way up the pyramid and ultimately begin to "create" your life the way you always dreamed and not controlled by conditioning.

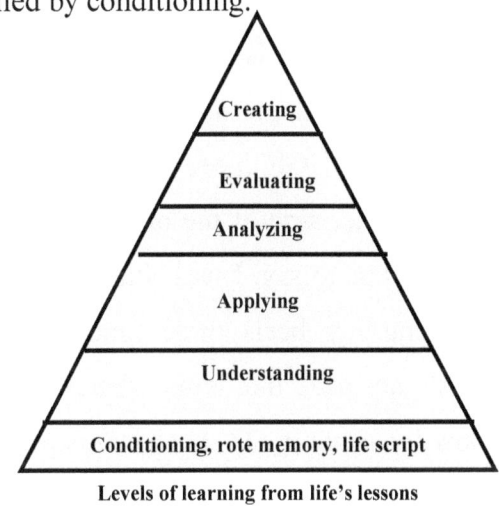

Levels of learning from life's lessons

We are all creatures conditioned to respond to external stimuli, the majority of the time reacting without thinking. It's a basic Pavlovian response or "classical conditioning" in psychological terms. Pavlov's classical conditioning is basically learning through associations. For example, I remember I had a deep fear of the dentist for many years because when I was young I had to get a shot of Novocain in the roof of my mouth. The dentist stuck the "HUGE" needle (to a kid it was huge…trust me) into the roof of my mouth and shot in the medicine.

Now you have to realize that this was way before topical anesthetics that they give you now before they stick in the needle. Ok, hang with me here…the needle is in the roof of my mouth and he goes on to move it, not remove it, but moves the needle as it is still stuck in the roof of my mouth over to another angle and shoots. Then he, again without pulling the "HUGE" needle out, proceeds to move the needle to the other side of the original needle opening and shoots. Needless to say, I was sitting there with white knuckles, clicking my heels three times and saying to myself, "there's no place like home, there's no place like home." I know I was not in OZ, but I was experiencing and now associating a visit to the dentist with "PAIN."

If you compare my dentist experience with the experience that my kids have had from the very start, the difference in learning through association is clear. They had a dentist whose office was decorated like a jungle with video games, stuffed animals, and tokens given to the kids after their visit. These tokens were good for a treat from the prize machine. You can see how their expectations or association with a visit to the dentist is completely different from mine. They are excited to go and have associated a dentist visit with fun and prizes. I had to work through my fear of the dentist and it wasn't until I found out that they had topical anesthetics that I felt comfortable going back.

We are constantly learning through association. We are always students of life, learning to react to the situations in this classroom of life. You continually learn or become conditioned by the stimuli you encounter each and every day. Sometimes people are mindful of their reactions and then try to control them. Unfortunately, some people go through life believing that they are "victims" of life instead of believing they can control what they feel, think, and how they behave. If you have the attitude that you are a "victim" you are not taking 100% responsibility for your life and your learning.

Seek Lessons + Participation in your learning = Active/Conscious Learner

In order to take 100% responsibility for your life's choices, you must become an active/conscious learner in the classroom of life. An active/conscious learner is one who seeks out the lessons to learn and is an active participant in the learning process. If you don't become an active learner, you will not learn what is needed for your spirit to grow and develop into the person you were meant to be. The choice is yours!

Be Mindful that you are a Teacher of Life:

At the same time that you are a student of life, you are also a teacher. You teach people how you see life and how to treat you. For example, if you still have the "victim" mentality, you are teaching people that you think life is not fair and how situations and people are against you. You are teaching people to treat you as a victim both by what you focus on and if you let them walk all over you. Remember, "You teach people how to treat you." They wouldn't walk all over you if you don't let them. The choice is yours!

Be Mindful that you have "freedom of choice"

"The strongest principle of growth lies in human choice."
- George Eliot

God has given each of us a great gift. This gift is the freedom to make choices. Unfortunately, some have not accepted this gift as their own. Some people don't believe that we truly have the freedom to choose and there are those who believe more in destiny than freedom of choice.

I have asked many of my classes and personal students whether they believe in freedom of choice or fate. They battle with finding an answer. I don't know if there is a definite answer either way. I do know that how you answer the question of fate vs. freedom of choice will determine the level of control you feel you have over life's circumstances. For example, if you believe you are controlled by fate or destiny alone and you have lived a life with tragedy or disappointment, you will more likely see yourself as a "victim" of life, powerless, and blaming everything on powers outside yourself. On the other hand, if you see your life's painful situations in terms of the choices you make and you take responsibility for your life, then you will have the power to make the changes you need to find peace and balance in your life.

We are constantly creating and recreating who we are and how we perceive ourselves through the choices we make in life. Each situation gives us the "opportunity" to express or manifest a part of our soul/spirit and all situations can be seen from more that one perspective. For example, if we find ourselves in a difficult or painful situation, we can choose to be a "victim" and be at the mercy of life's situations or we can choose to see life's situations as lessons meant for us to learn what we need to find peace and balance in life. Ultimately it is our choice! What will you choose?

Be Mindful of your "Energy Investments"

Before getting into the three steps, let me talk a little about your energy investments. First, imagine the energy you have within you as cash or an asset. Each day you have a choice on where you want to spend your energy. You are only allotted a certain amount of energy per day and you need to be wise as to where you will invest it.

Just like the investment world, there are so many places where you can put your cash that it can be difficult to decide. With every investment there will be risk involved and this must be taken into consideration before giving your money. The same goes for your energy investments as well. For example, in the stock market you can buy a stock, let's say Walmart. If the Walmart stock goes up, you will get some return on your money. This is good. You just made more money. But if the stock starts to go down and you are losing money, then the wise thing is to sell before you lose it all.

Now this is a bit simplistic when discussing financial matters, but it is a good illustration of how we have and make energy investments everyday. For example, ask yourself where are you spending your time or assets? Is this task or activity giving you more energy and lifting you up or is it draining you of your energy? If it is draining you of your energy, then it, like the stock, is losing you money and it is time to sell or spend less time doing that activity. If you enjoy working out, listening to certain types of music, going to church, or just watching movies and you feel re-energized or rested, then that would be a good investment of your energy. Negative investments of your energy would result in you feeling that you are "hitting your head against the wall" or you just feel drained of your energy.

The amount of risk that you can accept in the financial world can correlate with the amount of risk that you can take in your personal energy investment world. There will be activities, like getting your higher education, which will take a lot of your energy with high risk, but the return will be enormous when you complete it. To chance loving, when your heart can be broken, is risky but the rewards could be great. The main point is to be aware of your "energy investments" and what kind of return on your energy you are getting back. If there are activities or thought that make you feel drained, identify them, stop doing them, and then choose a better investment vehicle for your energy. The choice is yours!

Energy Investment Exercise

Write down the activities or places you "spend" your time & check whether or not you get a positive return or negative return on your time.

Your energy investments:	+	−
For Example: going to church, having coffee with a friend	+	
Being around negative people, thinking negatively, worry, etc.		−

Step #1:
"Become Mindful of Your Personal Boundaries & Responsibilities"

"The Concept of 3"
"Focus on what you <u>truly</u> have control over: What you <u>think</u>, <u>feel</u>, and how you <u>behave</u>."

Ok…here we go…Repeat this to yourself over and over: "There are only three things that I can <u>truly</u> control in this world…"
1) How *I* think.
2) How *I* feel.
3) How *I* behave/react.

"That's it. I cannot <u>truly</u> control how anyone else feels, behaves, or thinks."

Ok, repeat this again and again, until it sticks in your mind and it becomes engrained!

<u>Understand that you can only control what "you" think, how "you" feel, and how "you" behave.</u>

Yep, that's it! The only things in this world you truly have control over are how you think, how you feel, and how you behave. That's it! Think about it. You really can't control how someone else thinks, feels, or behaves. Oh yes, you may try and yes you may have some influence on their decisions, but ultimately they are in control of how they think, feel, and behave. Not you! A perfect example is the old psychologist joke…"How many therapists does it take to change a light bulb? One, but the light bulb has to "want" to change." Just like a person who is an alcoholic or addict, no matter how much you try to change the way they think, feel, or behave, ultimately they have to "want" to change. Yes, you can do an intervention, but it is their choice to learn, not yours. All you can do is offer the opportunity to learn and grow by disseminating information. The ultimate choice to learn is their's alone.

So why even try to "control" what someone else thinks, feels, or behaves? Many times we feel the need to control others or the situations we find ourselves. This need is because we ourselves feel out of control. We fail to focus on where the control should be placed…**"On Us!"** A great example of this is when I was working as a therapist in Pasadena and I had a client's family in for a family session. My client was a 5 year old child taken from the home because of abuse issues and he was the middle of 5 kids. During the session, I noticed his mother was busy going from one child to another trying to keep them in order, but in my opinion they were behaving fine. I watched as she tried to control their interactions, feelings, and behaviors.

I brought this up to my supervisor afterwards and she said that it all makes sense. I said…"Ok, explain why this mother had to be in everyone's business." She said that the mother was so busy trying to control the other family members, that if she didn't, she would have to stop and sit still…which means that she would have to focus on "her" issues and not the issues of the other family members. So the mother was so busy trying to control others because she was afraid that if she stopped, then she would have to deal with her own issues. Interesting huh?

Ask yourself, do you do that? Do you have to control or be involved in the problems of others? Do you complain about how others behave, think, or feel? If so, then ask yourself why and what are you getting out of this need to control or complain? Remember, "Every behavior has a purpose to it…we wouldn't be doing it if we didn't get something out of it." I am not saying don't care about someone and try to help them with their problems. I am saying that you must know where to draw the line between your "need" to control and the "self-determination" or "freedom of choice" of the other person. If you stop trying to control the feelings, thoughts, and behaviors of others around you and instead focus on controlling your own feelings, thoughts, and behaviors, then life becomes less stressful and more manageable. It's all about being mindful of your responsibilities and drawing appropriate boundaries in your life. The Choice is yours!

Most people understand that we can control our behaviors, but it is much harder to understand how we might have control over our thoughts and feelings. You may be saying to yourself, "my thoughts and my feelings just happen, "I can't control them." Well, it is true that we can't completely control all of the thoughts and feelings that we experience. If so, we would be Vulcan (for you Star Trek fans out there). For those of you who are not Star Trek fans, the Vulcans are aliens from another planet who have learned how to control their emotions and their thoughts. We have literally hundreds of thousands of thoughts and feelings per day and some thoughts come into mind randomly and without warning. The Vulcans focus on logic and reason alone and see their emotions as unnecessary. They have developed techniques which help to suppress their emotions because they believe that if unchecked, emotions can cause damage. It is not that they are without emotions at all, but they have learned how to suppress them completely and choose to live without showing emotions.

Fortunately, we have not consciously developed techniques to help suppress our thoughts and emotions. I think that suppressing thoughts and emotions to the extent that a Vulcan would suppress their feelings is unhealthy. Feelings give us the flavors of life. They are the things that remind us that we are ALIVE! We should never be afraid of feeling emotions. Our feelings are neither good or bad, they just are; it's what you do with them that are important. What I want to emphasize is the need to acknowledge our feelings and thoughts. Only we can control which thoughts and feelings we are going to focus on and which ones we want to replace. We can also control whether or not we let our thoughts and feelings effect our behaviors.

You can control your behavior as well as your thoughts and feelings, but you cannot control how anyone else thinks, feels, and behaves. This is a very important concept to understand and to make a part of your thinking. When you understand the limits of what is truly in your control, you find that the things you normally would worry about, like what others think about you, will take up less mental time and energy. The Choice is yours!

The Savior Syndrome

Have you ever felt that if someone is unhappy, then you feel it is your responsibility to see that they are happy or you will do whatever it takes to make sure they are happy or fix it for them? Yes that's right, you may have the "Savior Syndrome." Many, especially mothers, nurses, therapists, teachers, or anyone in the Helping Professions, tend to have this "Savior Syndrome." You feel that if someone close to you is not happy, then you can "Save" them from their unhappiness or solve their problems. You take on the "responsibility" for their happiness. Remember, it is not your responsibility to make people happy! They are responsible for their own happiness. No one can make you happy or angry without your permission.

A good buddy and I once questioned the women in our master's program as to why so many women were attracted to guys that treat them like garbage and the nice guys, like us, were overlooked. Now, I understood that I was not the greatest looking guy in the world, but I also was not ugly. Brad Pitt I am not, but I am no Pee Wee Herman either. As for my friend, he was much better looking than average and he thought the same way. So we questioned, "why is it that the nice guys like us, who lady's magazines always say are the type of guys that women are looking for in a serious relationship, are being passed up for the "bad" boys?" We were learning to be therapists who are in touch with our feelings (one important characteristic women say they want in a man) and we were good listeners (another characteristic that seems important).

The answers we got from the ladies in our class, (and this has been supported by my female students all these years of asking this same question), was that the "bad" boys are a "challenge" and the nice guys are not. They seem to be a challenge to the women who have the mindset that "Ah, he wouldn't be that way if he only had a good woman; me," "he needs me" and "I can change him" or "save him from his negative ways and make him a good person." You may disagree with this assessment, but if you are this type of woman, ask yourself why you stay with that person who treats you like garbage. Are you trying to be his "savior?" Be honest with yourself!

Are You a People Pleaser?

Do you feel uncomfortable or uneasy when people are upset at you and will do anything not to cause friction? Do you fear confrontation because you are worried about how the other person will react? If you answered "Yes" to any of the questions above, you may be a "people pleasers." "People Pleasers" are those who would rather keep their feelings inside instead of confronting the person with whom they are having problems. They would rather die or beat themselves up than express their feelings of displeasure to the person with whom they have issues.

Some people pleasers place the needs of others before their own in hopes of getting noticed and lifted by praise from others, otherwise known as a martyr. The people pleasers sense of value is based on what other people think of them rather than what they think of themselves. By allowing others to define their value or by searching for approval from them, the people pleaser gives up power to others. This power, if in the wrong hands, can lead to manipulation, exploitation, or even destruction of the people pleaser's self-esteem and/or identity. Remember, **"No one can die your death, so don't let them live your life!"**

"None of us are responsible for all the things that happen to us, but we are responsible for the way we act when they do happen."
- Author Unknown

Knowing your boundaries and responsibilities help to reduce your stress and maintain balance in life and work.

You're only responsible for how you feel, think, and behave…that's it!

<u>*Personal Boundaries Exercise*</u>
Repeat to yourself again and again and again!

"There are only three things that I can truly control in this world…"
1) What *I* think.
2) How *I* feel.
3) How *I* behave/react.

"That's it. I cannot truly control anyone else's feelings, behaviors, and thoughts."
Repeat until it sticks and you can say it in your sleep!!

Step #2:
"Become Mindful of the "Energy Vampires" in Your Life."

Beware of the "Energy Vampires" in your life, they will suck you dry if you let them!"
Remember: You teach people how to treat you!

What are energy vampires & Who are your "Energy Vampires?"

Who are these "Energy Vampires" and how do I recognize them? While I worked as a Psychotherapist, I learned about and experienced the effects of "Energy Vampires." For me, energy vampires were clients who would leave me feeling totally drained of all energy by the end of our session. I would feel weak and emotionally sucked dry. Energy vampires are pessimists. One type of energy vampire I call the "Yes, But" Person. A "yes, but" person is someone who responds to any and all suggestions to improve their life by saying, "yeah, but (add any excuse here)." They like feeling sorry for themselves and want others to feel sorry for them as well. This is only one of several types of "Energy Vampire" you may encounter.

Another type of energy vampire is the totally negative person who continually complains and complains and complains. Have you ever had someone you know who was so negative that they drained you of your energy? You may have not even realized their effect on you at the time they were with you, but later you may have felt tired, weak or drained. These energy vampires suck your spiritual energy from you because they don't have their own spiritual energy. They are so empty that they need to suck off other's spiritual energy to feel normal. Identifying the energy vampires in your life and choosing to keep them from draining you of your spiritual energy is very important to reaching and maintaining balance in mind, body, and spirit. Again, the choice is yours!

Who or what is draining you of your energy or spirit?

The first step to becoming more mindful of the "Energy Vampires" in your life is to take an assessment of the people you hang around with the most, or the situations you tend to find yourself. Jack Canfield (2000), the author of "Success Principles" and the "Chicken Soup for the Soul" Series talked about how you are the average of the 5 people you hang around with the most. He explained that if three out of the five people you have contact with on a regular basis are negative, then you will more likely pick-up on their negativity and become negative. The same is true if more than three of the five people in your life are positive, you will become more positive. Mr. Canfield asked his professor, who was explaining this concept, that even if his mother was a negative person then he shouldn't hang around her? His professor said "Yes, you don't have to hang around them." I agree that you are not obligated to be around negative people, even if they are family.

Many of us feel obligated to spend time with loved ones who drain the spiritual energy from us. But what if they are so toxic that, like an acid, every time you come in contact with them it burns a hole in your soul? Do you still see them or feel obligated to spend time with them? What if you are not spiritually or mentally strong enough to deal with them? Should you still spend time with them? I say NO! Look at it this way. If you were sick and had a weak immune system, you would not go visit someone with a serious illness like Tuberculosis or the flu. You would wait until your immune system is stronger and able to fight off any other sicknesses that might be floating around. This is the same thing you must do when you are dealing with a person who has the "spiritually illness of negativity." If your "spiritual immune system" is weak or not strong enough to fight off any "negativity disease" or "dis-ease," then you will become more susceptible to catching the "negativity disease" or to having your "spiritual immune system" weakened to the point of collapse.

Even if your "spiritual immune system" is strong, you will still want to minimize your contact with toxic exposures and diseases. What do we do when we're going into a disease infested area? We get inoculated and take other precautions to minimize the risk of catching the "disease." The same holds true here when you are planning to visit that relative with the "negativity dis-ease." Lets say you have to pay a visit over Christmas or any other family holiday and a negative family member will be there. You can prepare your "spiritual and mental immune system" like you would if you were getting ready to travel to a disease infested country.

Plan Your Reaction

I recommend that you practice deep breathing techniques and positive mental mantras, which are words of concentration that help to protect the mind, such as "this too shall pass" or repeat "the three things I can control." Also, by practicing these techniques you will be better able to react to the negativity so that the negative energy does not linger and stick to you when you leave. Plan your reaction! If you are a couple and have negative in-laws, you can support each other with a plan of action (like a tap on the leg as a reminder to breathe) when confronted by the "negatively ill" person. This technique can also be used at office parties, get-togethers, or any place that you know there could be the chance of catching the "negativity bug." The more practice you get the better you become at warding off the negativity with **"Spiritual & Mental Booster Shots."** The choice is yours!

External Energy Drains

Throughout our travels in this life, we all encounter people and situations that can be considered negative. People who get in the way of what we are working towards or external frustrations that trip us up from time to time that drain our spiritual energy. Traffic is a good example of an external energy drain. How many of us get frustrated at a traffic jam or a slow down in the traffic flow, especially when we are running late for an appointment? Yes, I too have allowed myself to get frustrated a time or two by the traffic I hit on the way to work. When I recognize that I am getting frustrated, I ask myself: "what part of this situation can I control?" If I can move into a faster moving lane, then I try that. If not, and the traffic is slow no matter which lane you are in, then I practice my deep breathing exercises and mental mantras. I like to remind myself that I can't get frustrated at the traffic because "I am the traffic." So I change my focus and take the time to look around at things on the side of the road or other cars that I normally would not have paid attention to because I would be flying by. If you find yourself caught in traffic or any other stressful situation, remember to breathe, focus on what you can and cannot control, and then change your focus onto something other than the external energy drain. Try it. It makes a big difference! The choice is yours.

Internal Energy Vampires

After assessing the external energy drains, you might find that it is not really external things and people that are frustrating and draining you of energy. Maybe the energy vampires come from you and your thoughts. For example, you just got out of a tough traffic drive or a tough day at work and you keep thinking about it, running it over and over in your mind. If you continue to complain about it or think about it over and over, you relive the whole experience without the external stimuli. It's your thoughts that are now draining you of your spiritual energy and your body. Hormones and your nervous system will react as if you were still stuck in traffic. Imagine that you had a disagreement with an in-law and you are so frustrated with what they said or did. You play it over and over in your head and you even talk to your spouse. You even lose sleep over it because you allow it to run on in your head. You are wasting energy! You have the choice to let the negativity get you down.

Unfortunately, when we are effected by the negative people in our lives they touch the negative parts of us which adds to the internal energy drain. The biggest sources of negative thoughts or feelings we may have inside are fears, insecurity and self-doubt. When we dwell on them they come to the surface and waste energy. Remember, your words, thoughts, and worry can be as big of a spiritual energy drain as the external frustrations. That is why it is important to remind yourself of what you can truly control: how you think, how you feel, and how you behave. That's it. If you try to control more than that, you are wasting valuable spiritual energy that could be used more wisely on positive things in your life. Remember, you can only control how you think, how you feel, and how you behave!

Beware of "Emotional Black Holes!"

There are some people who are considered "emotional black holes." These are people, like a black hole in space, who are basically dark, and empty. If you get to close, their gravitational pull will suck you into their negativity. They are the really negative people or situations that have no bottom and no matter how much you try, they will never feel full or happy or at peace. They like to bring people down and thrive on negativism. They will always find the gray lining in every white cloud. They are emotionally empty and must be avoided at all cost. If not, then you will find yourself sucked into their problems and feeling your energy sucked out of you.

Another way of recognizing the emotional black holes is to look into their eyes. Normally you can look into someone's eyes and see a bit of a spark, but for the emotional black holes, there is no spark at all. In some, you can only see a deep creepy kind of darkness. It is like there is not a conscience or any spirit or soul within them. This emptiness seen in the eyes is another way to recognize the emotional black holes. When you come in contact with someone like this, for your sake and the sake of your mental, physical, and especially your emotional/spiritual well being, identify the "emotional black holes" and run, don't walk, as fast as you can away from them. They are not worth losing yourself or your energy! The choice is yours!

What does Your Personal Energy Universe Look Like Exercise.

Imagine yourself as a planet just like the planet earth with an atmosphere, natural resources (water, land, etc), pollution, inhabitants, and even wars. You are a planet that is self sustaining and able to sustain life. There are storms, hurricanes, deserts, and wetlands. You are the center of "your" universe and you also have other planets with the same characteristics or planetary atmosphere and natural resources as your own. They have an atmosphere, natural resources, pollution, inhabitants, storms, wars, etc. but they are in orbit around you. These are the people or planets that you have the most contact with during your day. They can also be those people who mean the most to you or are major players in your life. So for the following exercise, I want you to identify 1) the major players in your life and 2) the people with whom you spend the most time.

First identify each individual person by using the "energy solar system diagram" below. Mark the middle circle as yourself and the first ring as the people you live with or the ones who you have the most contact with during your day. Use the next ring for those who you see sometimes and the outer rings for those you rarely interact with and so forth. Next I want you to identify the "Energy Vampires" in your life by marking the positive ones with a (+) and negative energy people in your life with a (-). See Example below.

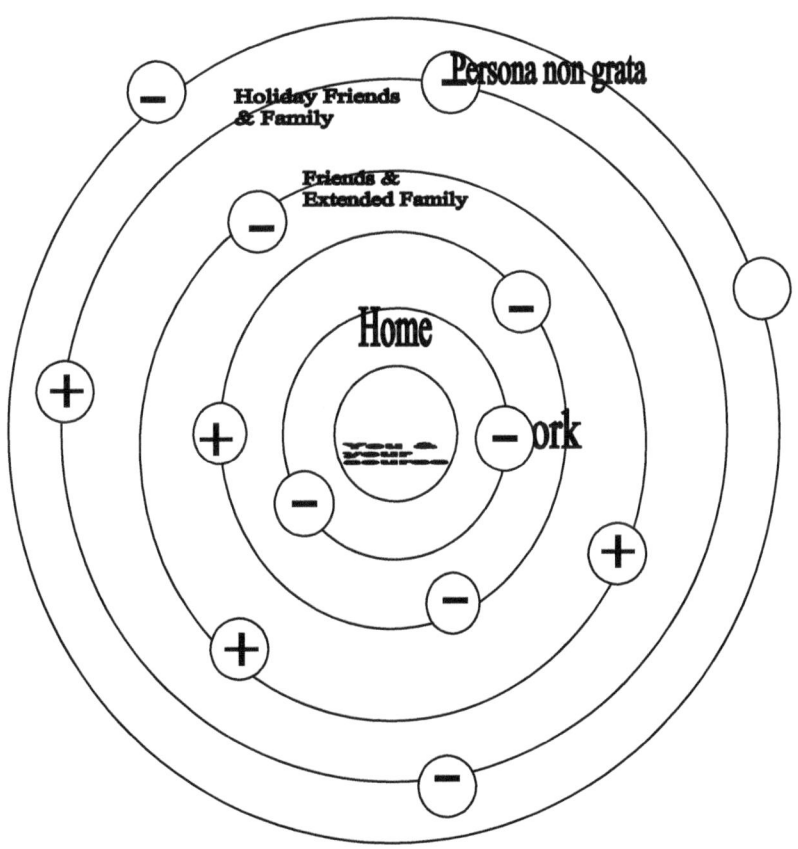

There are times when you have planets colliding and sometimes we find wars of the worlds happening in our universe. Sometimes we will have some planets that come into orbit and then out of orbit. These are friends who come into our lives for just a moment in time to touch us and leave a little bit of themselves with us. Now understand that the people who are in orbit with you do not have to be in your orbit. You can move the negative people to the outer limits of your universe. In this case, you are the master of your universe and can choose who gets the privilege of being in the "inner circle" of your universe. Who shall it be? The choice is yours!

Time to describe your "Personal Energy Universe"

Use the following chart to map out the positive and negative people in your universe. Remember that you can move any negative person to the outer ring. You are not "obligated" to sacrifice your personal energy for the sake of anyone, unless you consciously choose to do so. Who will you choose to move into your inner energy circle or move out to the persona non grata realm?

Exercise #1:
Your Personal Energy Universe

First identify each individual person by using the "energy solar system diagram" below. Mark the middle circle as yourself and the first ring as the people you live with or the ones who you have the most contact with during your day. Use the next ring for those who you see sometimes and the outer rings for those you rarely interact with and so forth. Next I want you to identify the "Energy Vampires" in your life by marking the positive ones with a (+) and negative energy people in your life with a (-).

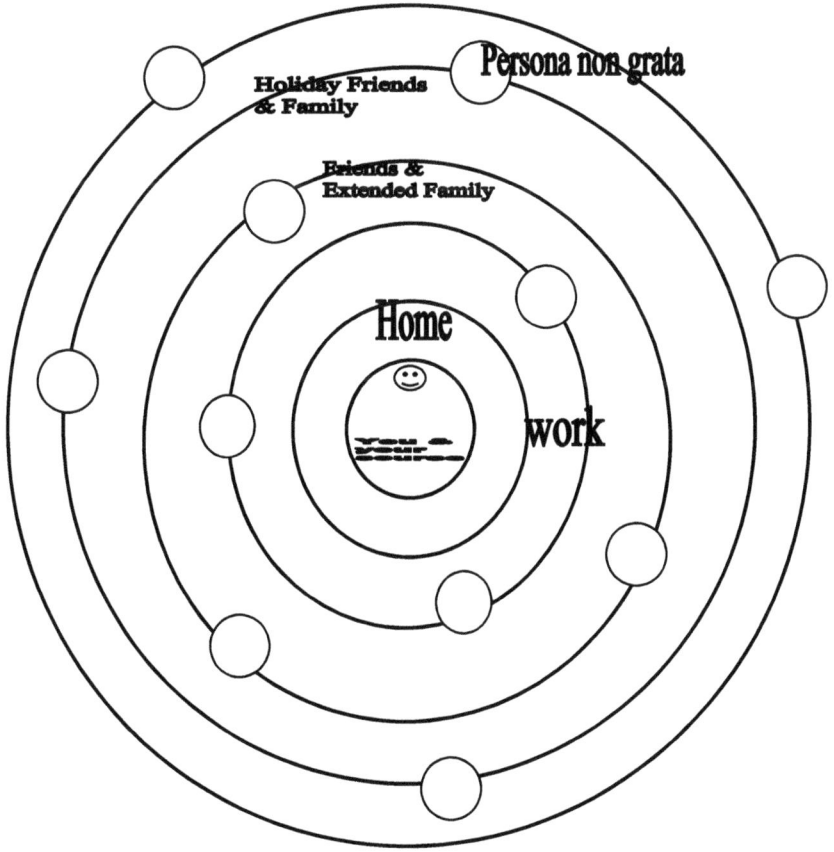

Use this to plot the energy vampires for your personal lives, activities, work environment, or any part of your life that needs specific evaluation. Using the same directions mentioned in the exercise, identify the energy vampires and the good energy investments in your life.

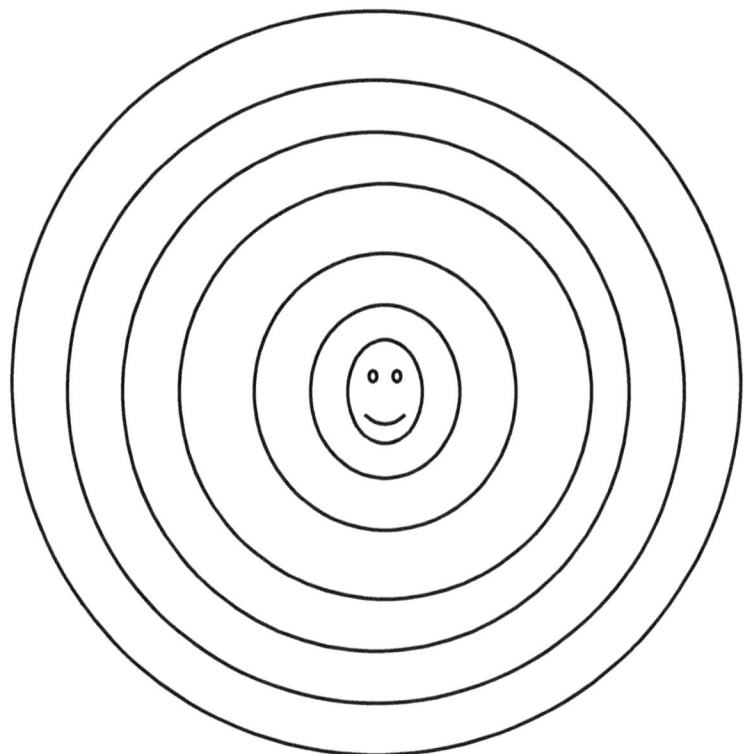

If life were a movie,
are you living your own drama or comedy?

Another way to look at your life is to see it as a movie. Do you see your life as a comedy, a drama, a mystery, or an adventure? Do you see each day as a comedy, drama, or as an adventure? If you see your life as a movie, you must realize that this is not a dress rehearsal. You are the playwright, lead actor, the producer, the director, and even the audience of this movie called life.

In this movie of your life, you must recognize and accept the fact that you are personally responsible for creating your movie each day of your life. You are not a victim of circumstances or the influence of others and you do have the ability to change your script or story. You must constantly ask yourself, "is this the way I want my movie to turn out?" If it isn't, you must be willing to take the actions necessary to make the changes needed to make the movie what you want.

You are a unique individual and each movie is just as unique. Your movie is the most authentic expression of who you truly are and the single most important act of creativity that is within your grasp. In this personal movie of life, you must live every scene and every line to the fullest with the awareness that the scenes you experience are of infinite value. Remember, each scene is performed only once and then never again, you must value each moment and experience as precious. The choice is yours!

If life were a movie, what kind of movie are you living right now? Would it be a comedy, drama, or action adventure? What kind of life would you want to live? Do the exercise below.

Exercise #2:
"Writing your own personal movie script!"

After reading the section above, answer this question: Using the information from "personal energy universe" exercise above, identify "who you would write out of your script or make a smaller part and why?

Remember: you are the script writer for your life and you get to write in or write out ANYONE you want or need to in order to find peace and balance in your life.

Steps#3:
"Become Mindful of Your Islands of Stability"

In times of crisis, you need to know where your "Islands of Stability" are to get you through.

See the storms in life as opportunities.

Imagine that you are on a ship at sea and encountering a storm. This is a storm like no other. This is a storm that rocks your boat from side to side and up and down. Your biggest fear is that a huge crashing wave will come over the side of your ship and you will find yourself overwhelmed by life's problems or stressors. You are just holding on by the skin of your teeth and then suddenly, in the distance, you see a light shining. You try to guide your ship towards the light but another wave strikes and takes you another direction. But you continue to look for the light shining in the distance and then you finally see it again and you adjust your sails to ride the waves towards the light. You finally come closer to the light and see that it is a light house and you see land! You breathe a sigh of relief as you come into the harbor to dock and rest from the storm. You have found "an Island of Stability" in your life where you can rest and recoup from the pounding you encountered on your journey through the storms of life.

In this journey called "Life," we all will go through storms of uncertainty and the unknown. We all feel the fear of that last huge wave hitting us and knocking us over one last time. That last wave could be an electric bill that was not paid, a spouse who is verbally abusive, or maybe just a minor fender bender you get into on the way to work. Whatever life situation or stressor that hits you, big or small, it all will add up if you don't find moments of respite. In stress management terms, this is called the "pile-up theory." The "Pile-up Theory" says that when you are doing too much then the stressors in your life will begin to pile-up until you cannot handle it anymore. For example, if you continuously live today's fast paced "doing it all" lifestyle and don't take a little time to rest, then you will eventually be overwhelmed and stressed out. Then you get a speeding ticket going home or flat tire…the final wave hitting you. When this happens, out comes the "Straw that broke the Camel's back" and puts you over the top.

We all need to have "Islands of Stability" to help us when we are feeling overwhelmed by life's stressors and difficulties. These Islands of Stability can be either external or internal. The external Islands of Stability can be your church or family where you can go and find refuge from the storm. Unfortunately, sometimes it is our family that creates the storm and difficulties in our lives. When this happens, you must look for places that give you peace, like the outdoors, the woods, a park, or the top of a mountain, a water source like a river or a water fountain, or outlets like exercise, karate and hobbies. You must find some place that you can consider your island of stability where you know what to expect and you don't have to keep your head above water. This is a place where you can stop and take a deep breath and just be…you don't have to do anything but "JUST BE;" a place where you don't have to put on a fake smile or any other façade. You can just be yourself, even if it is for only a few minutes or hours. That's all it takes sometimes to get you back on your feet and re-center. Remember, even in nature, no storm lasts forever!

Identify the positive people in your life

Identifying the positive people in your universe is important when you find yourself in the middle of an emotional or situational storm. These are the people who are optimists and see or look for the silver lining in any difficult situation. These people will not suck you dry of your energy by bringing up all the negatives of the situation. Instead, they will help to lift you and your spirit up by accepting, encouraging, and helping you through your life's storm. They help to remind you that there is "hope" in all difficult situations. These are true friends and you should keep them close to you, not only in difficult times, but all times. These are people whom you can go to, be yourself with, and who will accept you unconditionally.

Exercise 3
Identify your "Islands of Stability"

Write down where your "Islands of Stability"
are for you to find rest.
If you can't think of any, begin by identifying some people
or places where you can go to re-center yourself.
Also identify why you like the Island of Stability.

External Islands of Stability

The positive people in your life are external islands of stability, but there are more that you can identify if you only look. For many, home can be an external island of stability or church can be a place where you can find a sense of acceptance or peace. For myself, since being in Karate for the past 3 years, I have found that both the people and the exercise serve as a stabilizing force when I feel out of balance or stressed out. It could be a quiet place in a park, on a mountain top, on your porch, on a beach, or driving down a quiet road. Wherever it is, this external island of stability should be a place where you can spend time with yourself and find peace and rest from the storms of life. Consider it your port to rest, recuperate, and reenergize.

Internal Islands of Stability

When the storms of life hit us hard, they don't only hit us from the outside. We often have "internal" storms raging as well as the "external" ones. It's the external frustrations, like bills, boss, children, etc., that are easy to recognize and can cause us to become out of balance causing internal storms to start up. These "internal" storms in our heads, heart, and souls are harder to identify. These are called "personal frustrations." In other words, there may not be an external storm going on around you but more of an "Internal Storm" that can be knocking you off balance.

Many times, it is the external situations or storms that cause the internal storms to start up. The internal storms are usually caused by insecurity, pride, or fear based on the way you are thinking or your conditioning. The internal storms consist of negative thinking or self-doubt that causes us to beat ourselves up mentally and emotionally. Waves of worry and fear of the unknown are major causes of internal storms and can be controlled by controlling your thinking. Become mindful of what you think and the negative thoughts that create the storms inside your head. Become mindful of how you think and remember, "Change the way you look at things, and the things you look at will change" – Wayne Dyer…so choose wisely!

So now what do you do when confronted by an energy vampire?

Here are some tips to remember when you find yourself in the presence of an energy vampire. **Please note:** since we all are different, not every tip will be appropriate for every person or situation. Yet, the first three tips are vital and should be used and practiced as your staring point for any situation in which you find yourself. The other tips can used and applied as needed.

Step 1) Recognize & identify the Energy Vampire.
Step 2) Remember to Breathe!
Step 3) Remember the "Concept of 3."

These are the core concepts that you must remind yourself of and commit to memory. The following tips will help you to be more mindful of the information covered in the book.

1) **<u>Be mindful that life is a classroom & you are a student of life.</u>**

The energy vampire you are confronting may be teaching you an important lesson to help in your spiritual growth. There are lessons to be learned from every situation and energy vampire. A lesson as small as the needing to "take care of yourself" or saying "NO."

2) **<u>Be mindful that you are a teacher of life and you teach people how to treat you!</u>**

If you recognize that an energy vampire is sucking you dry with their negativity and don't do anything about it, you are to blame for your loss of life force.

3) **<u>Be mindful that you have the "Freedom to Choose."</u>**

You are not a victim of your circumstances and every situation gives you the opportunity to "choose" how you are going to react and how you are going to let the energy vampire effect you!

4) **<u>Be mindful of your "Energy Investments."</u>**

Choose where you invest your energy resources. You don't want to put good money or energy into something that will not pay you back with interest. Energy vampires are bad investment choices.

5) **Be mindful of your personal boundaries & responsibilities: The Concept of 3!**

Remember you can only control how you think, feel, and behave/react to the energy vampires. Don't be a savior or people pleaser. You will only get sucked into their web of despair.

6) **Be mindful of the internal and external Energy Vampires in your life.**

"Don't should-of all over yourself." Just because you make mistakes in life doesn't mean you have to beat yourself up about it. Forgiving yourself will help get rid of your internal energy vampires and blessing others will help get rid of the external energy vampires in your life.

7) **Be mindful of planning your reactions to upcoming encounters with energy vampires.**

If you know that you are going into a stressful situation where energy vampires will be, plan your reactions and escape plan. Play possible scenarios in your head step by step or talk it out with a friend, but make sure that your thoughts don't turn to worry. Worrying is the worst kind of internal energy vampire there is. Always start with the mindset that "this will be a fun leaning experience or an opportunity to practice your energy vampire defenses." Then end your mental preparation with blessing the potential energy vampire.

**The Beginning of a Life of Learning –
4 years old on the first day of Head Start!**

About the Author

Steve Ornelas is currently a Professor of Psychology and Life Skills Consultant/Coach focusing on Personal and Social Adjustment issues, Stress Management, and Self-Improvement Techniques for balancing Mind, Body, and Spirit. Dr. Ornelas' stated mission is to "Open Hearts and Minds" through quality educational opportunities for individuals and groups through "Learning made Fun" workshops and seminars.

Dr. Ornelas started his life of education at the early age of 4 when he attended the Head Start program near his home. Since then, he has received his Bachelors degree from the University of Arizona, Master's Degree from the University of Los Angeles California, and Ph.D. from Arizona State University. He also received a Massage Technician Certification from the Institute of Psycho-Structural Balancing in Santa Monica California. Dr.

Ornelas believes that life is a classroom with learning that can be found in every situation.

Dr. Ornelas has received the following distinctions: the CSWE Minority Fellowship Award, the David Pierce Workforce Teaching Leadership Award from the National Institute for Staff & Organizational Development (NISOD), Faculty Senate President at Central Arizona College, Who's Who among America's Teachers for 3 separate years, and the George Fridell Award for Teaching Excellence. Dr. Ornelas has earned his 2nd Degree Black Belt and is currently in training to become a Nationally Certified Instructor for the American Taekwondo Association (ATA).

In addition to the over 13 years of fulltime teaching experience, Dr. Ornelas has worked as a Psychotherapist with abused children and their families and currently has a private practice helping individuals to become more mindful of their life's lessons and finding balance in mind, body, and spirit.

Recommended Reading

Dr. Cherie Carter-Scott. excerpted from *Negaholics: How to overcome negativity and Turn Your Life Around* by Dr. Cherie Carter-Scott, Ballantine wellspring, original publication date, 1989. www.drcherie.com

Jack Canfield's "Success Principles." (2005). HarperCollins Publishers Inc. New York, NY. 10022
www.successprinciples.com

Dr. Wayne Dyer's books including: "The Power of Intention," "10 Secrets for Success and Inner Peace," and "There is a Spiritual Solution to Every Problem." Hay House, Inc. P.O. Box 5100 Carlsbad, CA 92018-5100
www.drwaynedyer.com

Sources

Dr. Cherie Carter-Scott. excerpted from *Negaholics: How to overcome negativity and Turn Your Life Around* by Dr. Cherie Carter-Scott, Ballantine wellspring, original publication date, 1989. www.drcherie.com

"Star Trek Deep Space 9": Episode 1 "Emissary": From Gene Roddenberry's *Star Trek* universe, created by Rick Berman and Michael Piller and produced by Paramount Pictures in 1993.

Forest Gump: Director: Robert Zemeckis . Main Cast: Tom Hanks, Robin Wright Penn, Gary Sinise, Mykelti Williamson, Sally Field. Paramount Pictures. Release Year: 1994 US

Gene Oliver (Former American Baseball player b1935). Found at http://thinkexist.com/quotes/gene_oliver

George Bernard Shaw. Quote Found at http://www.quotationspage.com/quotes/George_Bernard_Shaw/

Anderson, L. W. and David R. Krathwohl, D. R., et al (2000) *A Taxonomy for Learning, Teaching, and Assessing: A Revision of Bloom's Taxonomy of Educational Objectives*. Allyn & Bacon.

John Cotton Dana. Quote found at http://thinkexist.com/quotation/who_dares_to_teach_must_never_cease_to_learn/210326.html

George Eliot. Quote found at http://www.quotationspage.com/quotes/George_Eliot/

Jim Rohn quote found in Jack Canfield's "Success Principles." (2005). HarperCollins Publishers Inc. New York, NY. 10022

Dr. Wayne Dyer. Quote from live seminar in Phoenix AZ in 2007.

NOTES

Created by
Dr. Ornelas M.S.W., Ph.D.
Copyright © 2007 All Rights Reserved.
GabSum Productions LLC.
<u>No reproduction without written permission.</u>

For more information about GabSum Productions LLC,

Life Coaching, or

<u>"Life's Little Box of Chocolates – Experience the Flavors of Life"</u>

Workshop Series

<u>Workshops include:</u>

1) "Energy Vampires: Managing Stress & Negative Thoughts in your Personal & Professional Life.
2) "Life Skills Coaching & Training" – "Learn to live & not just exist"
3) "The Mind" – "Controlling the mental world of negative thoughts"
4) "Stress Management & Reflexology" – "Listen to the Messages from your body in times of stress"
5) "Spiritual Investments" – "Learn how to keep the Energy Vampires in your life from draining your spiritual energy"
6) "Relationships" – "can't we just get along?"
7) "Personal Self-defense" – "I'm no Victim – Find the confidence within"

To ask how you can order books or
to schedule workshops for your fund raising events
Call 602-550-8648 or email: sornelasphd@msn.com
To buy this book go to www.lulu.com/sornelasphd

www.ingramcontent.com/pod-product-compliance
Ingram Content Group UK Ltd.
Pitfield, Milton Keynes, MK11 3LW, UK
UKHW041433180426
11947UKWH00007B/423